AF522630

Aamir Khan

Actor With A Difference

Published in 2002 by

Rupa & Co

7/16, Ansari Road, Daryaganj
New Delhi 110 002

Sales Centres:
Allahabad Bangalore Chandigarh Chennai
Dehradun Hyderabad Jaipur Kathmandu
Kolkata Ludhiana Mumbai Pune

Photographs courtesy: Husain family

Cover & Book Design by
Arrt Creations
45 Nehru Apts, Kalkaji, New Delhi 110 019

Printed in India by
Gopsons Papers Ltd
A-14 Sector 60
Noida 201 301

Aamir Khan

Actor With A Difference

Lata Khubchandani

Rupa & Co

Aamir as 'Bhuvan' in 'Lagaan'

CONTENTS

Introduction

A fair, chubby, attractive four-year-old stands on a stool, leaning out of his balcony. He is intent on flinging something out with great vigour. His mother catches him in the act and discovers what he is throwing. Ten paise coins which the Indian government has recently issued — small with a rather cheap aluminium look. They obviously do not meet with the child's approval. His mother asks him *"Kyon phaink rahe ho?"* [Why are you throwing them?] He dusts his hands with satisfaction and announces *"Yeh bekar hain!"* [these are useless]

This is perhaps to set the tone for what the kid is about to grow up to be — an adult who dislikes all *'bekar'* [useless] things. It's a word that he is to use often in later life. After establishing himself as a popular filmstar, he uses this adjective to describe all the popular film awards. *"Yeh sab bekar hain!"*

He wants substance. Not fluff. He has no time for nonsense.

He is the second child of producer Tahir and Zeenat Husain. He is the child who will grow up to be the well loved film star Aamir Khan.

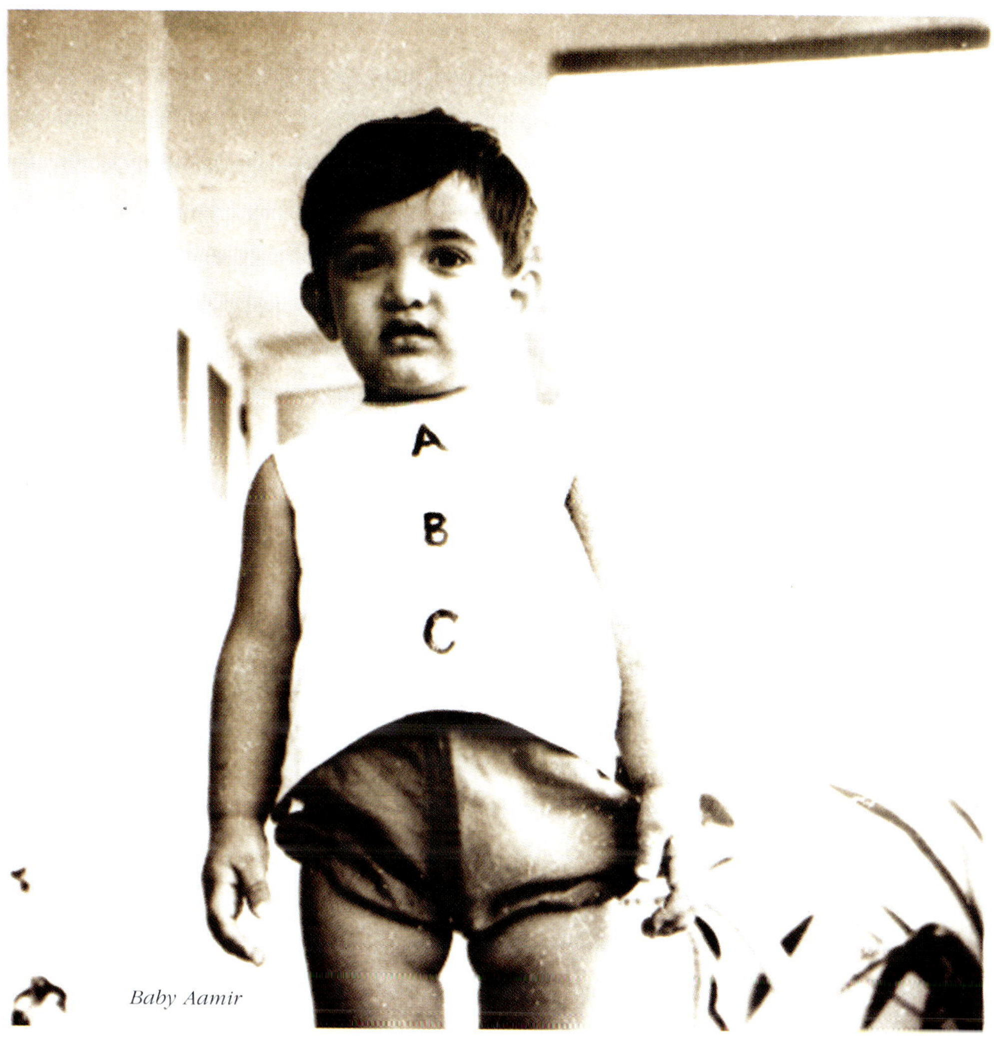

Baby Aamir

An analysis of Aamir Khan might superficially show nothing out of the ordinary, except perhaps the fact that he cultivates 'ordinariness' with a vengeance. And in a leading filmstar who sits atop a whole industry, that in itself is extraordinary. By this emphasis on not taking on the fluff that goes with stardom, Aamir has often irked his co-stars and peers. But he is adamant in his stand. The saving grace here is that he does not judge or misjudge his peers for doing just the opposite. He has never, in the fourteen years that he has spent as part of the film industry, tried to convert others to his way of thinking. But continues his rather lone crusade against the nonsensical trappings and misbehaviour of stardom.

Did I say he was ordinary? I was wrong. In a climate where the most common, the most average achiever underlines his achievement, Aamir Khan will always be an individual who stands alone, if not often isolated.

Chapter One

Early Years

"Even before he was born, my husband had chosen his name, Aamir. This means one who leads, one who bears the flag," recalled mother Zeenat. "He was always an exceptionally intent child. He wanted to try out everything himself and would insist on doing everything for himself. When he was very little, he'd put on his shoes and if we offered to tie his shoe laces he'd refuse to let us touch them. He'd bend down and try to tie them till he achieved it. If he wore a shirt and was struggling with the buttons, he'd be mortified if we tried to help him! A little later as he grew up, if he broke a button, he'd even sew it on himself!"

Aamir Khan was born on March14, 1965. Different, almost contradictory qualities of the child were surfacing in his early years. For the most part he was rather quiet, not too sociable, seemed almost shy. But with his brother Faisal, and sisters Nikhat and Farhat and cousins Nuzat and Mansoor, he was unusually demonstrative, very talkative, very dominating and

With mother Zeenat Begum

often a bully. He would order them about, lead them into scrapes and make them do his bidding.

He says grinning, "I loved to lie on my bed and read. I had this habit of making a mound of jam sandwiches and carrying them into my bedroom and reading comics and books borrowed from a circulating library. I'd spend almost my whole pocket money on this. After eating all those sandwiches I'd be thirsty, so I'd call Faisal and Farhat and announce 'let's see who can run faster and bring me a glass of water'. And they'd both shoot out of the room to the kitchen and fetch me water! This would work like a dream till it dawned on them that they were being had. Then they'd get mad!" And Aamir would have to rack his brains to find other ways to make them do his bidding.

Farhat, younger to Aamir by four years said, "He was always bullying me but he always did it so nicely. He'd say 'you're very sweet, go get me a glass of water' and I'd fall for it all the time. As I grew up I started complaining to mum that he was treating me like an errand boy. But mum would always be on his side. She'd say 'what does it matter, he's your elder brother, he's only asking for water, giving water to anyone is a good deed [*sawab*] go get it for him'."

With father Tahir Husain

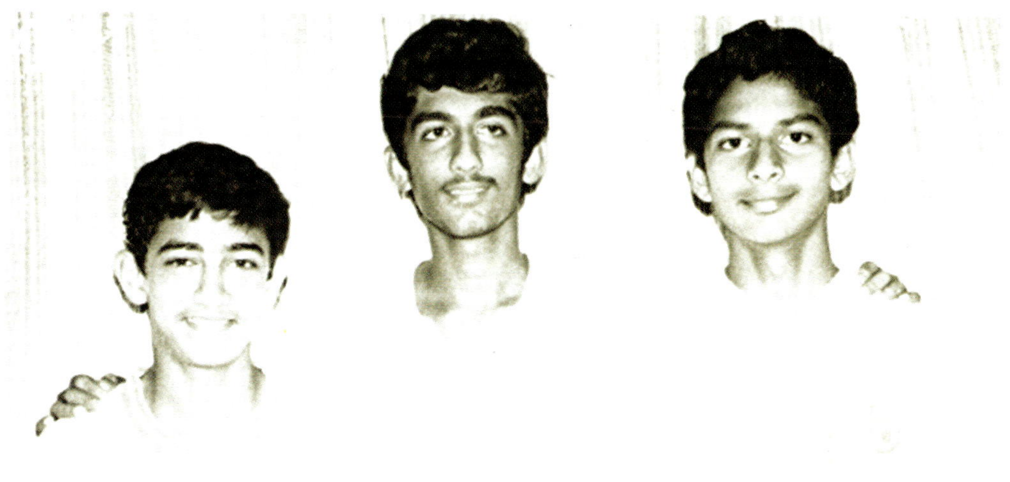

Aamir with his tennis mates

"Tennis", said father Tahir Husain, "was his biggest passion at one time; in fact he's always had something he was collecting or working on all the time. If he wasn't collecting coins, it would be marbles, then he was into tennis. He excelled at it and used to play at the Khar Gymkhana. Whatever he did, he kept on doing it till he mastered it so we knew that he would do anything well. He even played at the National level, he was so good."

Director Ashutosh Gowarikar vouched for this — though with much chagrin. "For tennis I'd go to the Khar gym and Aamir was already playing there since three years or so. He was the under 14 or under 12 champ, he was playing at a very high level. The first time I met him was at three in the afternoon, I'd reached the gym a little early. Aamir was knocking on the wall on his own because no one else was there. I told him, 'Come let's play'. He looked at me and said, 'No if I play with you I'll spoil my game.' I ignored it thinking this guy is really snooty.

But later when his partner came and I saw him playing I realised what he was saying was probably true, because his game was really perfect. While mine was ... well ... I didn't know how to control the ball yet. We were about twelve years old then and his mastery over the game was something to watch."

The young Aamir always had more girlfriends than boyfriends. "He'd always bring home his girlfriends and we used to have a private joke," said his grand aunt who has all but brought up Aamir from infancy. "I used to tell his mother jokingly, 'here comes Kanhaiyalal' because he always had these *gopis* around him."

Aamir in forefront with cousins and friends

This love/hate relationship with girls probably began from the time he was admitted into a girls' school because it was close to his house and it admitted boys up to the primary section. Here he was always arguing with the girls. He was so adamant about proving his point to them that his teacher once called his mother and advised her to enroll him into a boys' school. "I went to school to meet the teacher and she took me to his class so I could see for myself

Aamir with his brother, sister, mother, and grand-aunt Zohra Begum

what he was up to." She stood and watched him. He was completely turned around in his seat and was arguing vehemently with a group of girls, completely oblivious to the fact that he was in class!

But the same boy was courtesy personified when it came to adults. Zeenat Husain reflected, "He had this quality from childhood, he'd try to get his point across but always politely. I'm very proud that no one has ever complained about him ever being discourteous. In fact he'd often carry it too far. Once when he was about three years old, he was taking part in the school sports and was in the running race. A lot of parents were attending the sports day and some ladies from our building too were present. When they saw Aamir, to encourage him, they shouted, 'C'mon Aamir, c'mon' and Aamir thinking they were beckoning to him, left the race and came towards them. With the result that the other contestants raced past him. He was furious later!"

The young Aamir was showing signs early in life which were to become pronounced characteristics later. His affection and loyalty to his friends is well known. As a child too he displayed this in no small measure. The boy was such an attractive child that his paternal uncle Nasir Husain often told his mother that he would cast him in a film as a child artiste. Then one day he was shooting for *Pyar Ka Mausam* starring Shashi Kapoor and needed a child to play the boy Shashi Kapoor. He asked for Aamir to be brought to the shoot. Aamir's mother dressed him up in new clothes and new shoes, and he was taken to the location. Here he had to sit in a car for the shot but he refused. The whole day passed with everybody present trying to cajole him. Even his mother was called to try and persuade him. Then Nasir Husain asked for Aamir's younger brother Faisal instead. Faisal gave the shot in a jiffy and returned home.

Later at night when Aamir was asked why he had refused to sit in the car he said, "I wanted to sit in Reena's car!" Reena, filmmaker Raj Khosla's daughter was his great friend. She lived in the same building and he did not want to be disloyal to her by sitting in anybody else's car but hers!!

Aamir's generosity, his sense of sharing and his curiosity were also being developed from childhood. He had this habit of saving all the Id and birthday gift money with his grand aunt all through his school days. One day he suddenly requested her to give him his money. When

With family

his mother asked him why he needed it all at one go, he replied, "This person [he named someone they knew] needs money very badly and I'm going to give it to him." Aamir's mother realised that the child was doing an act of kindness and made sure he got all his money. Years later this generosity has got him fleeced often but that has not changed his magnanimous nature.

In Aamir, one sees a curiosity which spurs him on to learn all the time. If anything interests him, he delves into it so minutely that after figuring it out himself he is able to explain it to others equally clearly. The boy now discovered that he liked to crack most things which presented a problem — be it playing chess or fixing the Rubik's Cube.

"Aamir was very good at doing it", recalled Farhat, "after he'd managed to crack it, his next endeavour was to see how fast he could do it. So he'd call me and tell me to time him. I'd do this a few times and then get bored. But he'd say 'see I'm going to break the world record at this and when I do that I'm going to say that my sister Farhat helped me!' I'd be so thrilled that I'd sit back and time him all over again!"

Every child wants to grow up fast, to take his own decisions, to be free of adult interference. This desire must have been more pronounced in the boy Aamir. He was always so clear about what he wanted to do, that leaving his life's decisions to others irked him, his values were clearly getting defined pretty early in life; right from the time he started to think, in fact. Aamir had a very clear perception of what was true for him, he may not have always been right but that did not stop him from being clear about his priorities. If he was wrong, he was well prepared to accept it. Yet he never dithered in taking decisions for fear of being wrong. All his decisions have been taken by him with great clarity and responsibility; be it wanting to quit formal education in favour of film direction or marrying a Hindu girl. In his book of principles nothing is condemnable except injustice and unfairness.

Though Aamir was formally educated only till the 12th standard, he is a voracious reader, in fact at no point of time is he not in the middle of some book. He confided, "As a small boy, I hated to study but loved going to school and did well in the exams. I didn't have to study much because I remembered everything the teachers said in class. I started reading Enid

Teenage Aamir

Blyton when I was barely six years old. I remember this book named *The Enchanted Wood* even now. I read Alfred Hitchcock, *Hardy Boys* and *Nancy Drew* with great enjoyment. I used to get twenty rupees as pocket money every month and I spent it all on books. We weren't really allowed to see too many films. We'd see a film maybe once in three or four months."

Aamir's sense of responsibility too showed up early in life. Perhaps that is the reason he does not engage in whimsical behaviour — so abundantly seen in film stars. He revealed, "I was pretty naughty as a kid but was also very responsible, for example, if my parents asked me to do something they could be sure I'd do it. I used to see that no one stepped out of the building compound when we played there as kids."

Newcomer Rani Mukherjee got a chance to act opposite Aamir in *Ghulam* and she found that his sense of responsibility extended itself to her in the most endearing way. "I was very shy, I'd never had a boyfriend and doing a romantic scene with 'The' Aamir Khan made me very self conscious. But he'd just pull up my chin and say 'look at me' so casually and easily that I gradually relaxed with him and could match him. I consider myself lucky that I worked with Aamir so early in my career. I consider him my teacher in many ways."

Director Vikram Bhatt agreed, "Aamir is a great team man. Very supportive, very patient, always willing to listen and always there when anyone needs him. He makes it abundantly clear that if he's required for anything, he's around. He'll work overtime patiently and do anything in his power for the betterment of the film he's doing."

Chapter Two

Meeting His Wife

The games played in the building compound were so earnest that it developed into a production by itself. All the children in the building complex got together and formed what came to be called the 'Time Pass Gang'. When Aamir was old enough, he quite naturally slid into the role of leader. And once a year the Time Pass Gang held a fair to which outsiders were allowed for the price of a ticket. This allowed them to collect funds and the fair became bigger and bigger each year till they started having stalls, eats, orchestrated music, games etc. The kids from the surrounding buildings too became members and it was here that the teenage Aamir met Reena Datta.

Reena, the daughter of the Bombay Manager of Air India, lived nearby and played with the kids from Aamir's building. Aamir, himself armed with a strong sense of humour was intrigued by the mostly quiet but often tongue in cheek one-liners by Reena. Her sense of humour matched his own but she, unlike other girls, was her own person. He often took her home and his family too noticed the sober girl who stood out amongst his other pals. Aamir's grand aunt started smelling something though no one else did. "I thought he was paying special attention to her." she revealed.

Aamir had by now decided that he wanted to become a director in films. The Pune Film Institute was the 'in' thing those days and he broached the subject to his mother. Aamir was always closer to his mother, his father was a strict disciplinarian and Aamir tried to keep out of his way as much as possible. "Aamir said that after the 12th standard he'd like to join the Pune Film Institute," recalled Zeenat Husain, "but we said 'no'. Aamir tried to explain that it was a government course and as good as anything else he might join so why were we being so adamant? But we insisted that he complete his studies first and then decide anything further. He was very disappointed but said *'karna to wohi hai jo aap kahenge...* [I'll do what you say, but...] do please let me join the institute'." Zeenat Husain's eyes crinkled in reflective amusement as she recalled the above words so expressive of both Aamir's obedience and persistence.

"Finally I told his father what the boy desired and he said if Aamir was so keen to enter films why go to the Pune Institute, let him join my brother, filmmaker Nasir Husain as assistant and learn the ropes of direction. He could get hands on experience right here. So Aamir joined my brother-in-law and became an assistant with him."

Here he showed interest in everything, while he was learning the ropes of direction, whether it was editing, dialogue writing or music recording. His uncle was very happy with him. Aamir was also going to college. Around this time Ketan Mehta was casting for *Holi* and he auditioned a number of students, among them Aamir and Ashutosh Gowarikar. He finalised them both. But he was to shoot in Pune so Aamir requested permission from his father to go to the shoot for the film. It was granted on condition that they shoot during the vacation. In the same way, he did *Raakh* during his holidays. He also worked with playwright Mahendra Joshi and did some theatre, thereby adding to his experience as both director and actor.

Meanwhile Nasir Husain found that his big starcast films were flopping badly. He then decided to make his next film with newcomers and started scouting around for fresh faces. After disappointing auditions with newcomers he suddenly noticed his nephew and assistant Aamir, realised that the boy was good looking and intelligent. He announced that he had decided to cast Aamir in his next film. And that he would speak to his parents the same day. It was decided that Nasir Husain would launch Aamir Khan and *Qayamat Se Qayamat Tak* was made.

Midway through the film, Aamir Khan and Reena Datta had a quiet, registered marriage. Aamir turned twenty-one in March 1986 and in April he got married secretly. Quietly and unequivocally asserting his adulthood and his right to make his own decisions.

The suddenness and secrecy of the marriage was necessitated by the fact that the two came from different backgrounds and were still to settle in life. Reena was still a student. Reena and Aamir already emotionally involved with each other, were afraid that Reena's parents might get her married to someone else. They got married but continued living in their respective houses without letting anybody in on their secret. Reena's sister Anju started smelling a rat and threatened to spill the beans to their father who was then away in Calcutta. Aamir requested Anju not to do anything so drastic but she was adamant. The guilty couple was in a dilemma. Reena's father was due back from Calcutta and Anju was ready with her story. Reena was frightened of his wrath but there seemed to be no solution, till Aamir decided that the time had come to break the news to his parents.

With Reena, on their wedding day

He collected his whole family including uncle Nasir Husain and his wife and together with Reena announced that they were married. Tahir Husain, to his eternal credit sized up the situation at once, hugged them, smiled and said, "Oh you have got married haven't you? Good." And he welcomed his new daughter-in-law. Aamir's mother though taken aback that her young, rather quiet son had taken such a big decision of life alone, also took it in her stride. Young Farhat always vocal, thought that Aamir was too young to decide such a thing so early in life but Aamir reassured her that he knew what he was doing and had done it with his eyes open.

The next problem was that Reena was not ready to face her father now that her secret was out, so her father-in-law said easily, "Let her stay here, we'll get clothes etcetera made for her. We accept her as our daughter-in-law from this moment itself." Meanwhile Anju kept phoning Aamir's house to ask her sister to return home. Reena was adamant in her refusal. Friends of Reena's father tried to cajole the girl back to her father's house but had to accept defeat.

The blissful newly weds

Mr Datta arrived from Calcutta and when he heard the news he was so furious that he became ill. He had to be admitted to a nearby hospital. The next day Aamir's parents told him he must go and see his father-in-law. Aamir not only visited him in hospital but was consideration personified. Seeing this Mr Datta was mollified. Then both their parents met and decided that perhaps the match was not as unwelcome as they might have initially supposed and things

settled down. To such an extent that Farhat, Aamir's youngest sister, later married Rajiv Datta, Reena's brother!

Aamir looks back upon this episode seriously enough. "I've always enjoyed women with a sense of humour and Reena had a great sense of humour. Once she was doing some experiment with a cockroach and munching something. I stood next to her and asked what she was eating? She replied 'an éclair, want one?' I said 'yes' and she said 'open your hand'. I did and she placed a cockroach in it! I think I lost my heart to her then!! Just think, she gives me a cockroach and I give her my heart!"

Marriage to Reena was probably what the doctor ordered. Aamir's first film *Qayamat Se Qayamat Tak* became a smash hit. Other offers came pouring in, though the media was skeptical about this very youthful, chocolate faced hero lasting for any considerable time in the tough film industry. Aamir was keen on working with other big banners and proving his versatility as an actor. A lot of small banners came to sign him up till he could prove himself. He continued living with his parents along with wife Reena who was going to college then. As soon as films started coming his way, he bought his first car, a Maruti 800 and his first flat in the same building complex where he had always lived and still does.

Chapter Three

Evolution of an Actor

A series of hits with a few misses proved that Aamir Khan was here to stay and he had established himself in no mean manner. Apart from fame and celebrity status, the actor was also working out in his agile mind — a kind of time table for himself, a code of rules as it were, about what his life and films should be about. After signing the first lot of films he realised that acting in a number of films at the same time was not an ideal way of working. He had finally entered a profession which he enjoyed and doing too many films simultaneously without getting time to savour his work was not his definition of enjoyment. He completed the lot he had signed and made it clear that he was unwilling to work on more than one film at a time.

The industry protested. The Hindi film industry as it exists in Mumbai has been proud of its 'no-rules whatsoever' rule for stars. Here the star is supreme and everyone else awaits his

Debuting in films

pleasure. This has over the years given rise to a reprehensible star system which allows a star every indulgence at the expense of the filmmaker, so that many a time filmmakers have been ruined by whimsical stars without any notion of discipline whatsoever. Aamir Khan has contributed in a large measure in reversing this regrettable system and making stars responsible for the expenditure and to a large extent, the fate of their films.

When he decided that he was not going to work in more than a single film at a time, it became essential that he choose this film with utmost care. In hindsight, one might say that Aamir

Khan was setting up for himself a procedure of choosing and doing films which had at least a larger chance of success than this industry has ever known. In an industry where bound scripts were considered a joke, today the trend is moving towards having fully written scripts. Stars who were notorious for coming late, staying away from shoots etc. have today realised that the kind of work Aamir Khan puts into every film allows him at least a semblance of success in that even if the film fails. No one can point a finger at the star's performance — his sincerity is so evident. He gives complete attention to the film he agrees to do, from the time the script is shown to him, till after the release of the film. He then hands over the film to the audiences for their verdict. And because he gives so much of himself to each film, his belief in it is complete.

Ironically the industry 'accuses' Aamir of professionalism, a quality which is usually seen as a virtue, is in him seen as a vice

He justified this, "See I'm very professional as far as my responsibilities go and in what is expected of me but I'm not professional when it gets down to achieving what is required to be achieved. Suppose I am expected to work eight hours a day but the shoot is not over and the eight hours are up and we still have to achieve the shot or scene. I will extend those eight hours to twelve or sixteen or whatever is required to finish what we set out to do. If I was strictly professional I'd say, sorry my eight hours are over I have to go, or sorry I'm just an actor why should I come and select which banner or website to put my film under? Once I'm doing a film I see it as my film and if the producer or director or anybody from the unit calls upon me to see what they're doing I'd love to do that. It doesn't bother me that it's eating into my time to do so. I think I'm an emotional person, I work emotionally, I give. But what is required of me professionally, from that point of view I'm very professional. And I would do this for every film because I enjoy working that way. I enjoy achieving the best possible result for whatever we are doing, whether we're making a film or doing an interview or playing a game of chess. I want to enjoy doing it to the fullest, so I don't want to compromise at that time."

Ace makeup artist Mickey Contractor threw light on this famed professionalism during the making of *Baazi*, "In *Baazi*, he had to don the guise of a female. To give him his cleavage I had taped him. When he had to take it off, Aamir thought that if he yanked it at one go it'd be better than taking it off slowly. In doing so, his entire skin came off but he didn't call off the shoot. The next day he used bandage and taped himself again because it was continuity. He's amazing. He must've been in excruciating pain but that wasn't enough justification for him to take time off till his skin healed. And it was hot too, he was sweating and through all that he continued." Ashley Rebello his designer in *Baazi* adds, "There's nothing false about him, nothing fake. He's genuine as a person — you know you can take him at face value."

In Baazi – *playing a girl*

Today he is one of the top stars in the Indian film industry but he has never become a victim of stardom. He sees his work as a job to be done with the greatest efficiency and meticulous care and having seen the results of this, his peers in the industry have started following his footsteps. Such is his reputation that he is, even among the top stars, the only one who is considered the distributor's darling. And the step ladder that newcomer directors use to heave themselves successfully into the industry.

For Aamir, acquiring this reputation of dependability was merely a matter of time, till others perceived what was for the star, a matter of fact routine. Directors, co-stars and others who worked with him discovered his high sense of integrity and responsibility and felt reassured by his presence in any project.

Ashutosh and Aamir

Ketan Mehta, who directed the amateur Aamir in his first film *Holi* recalled the intense, young actor, "He was very young, still studying in college. My film *Holi* was about one day in a college campus. I was looking for totally fresh faces who had never acted in a film before and I met Aamir through my theatre contacts. I gathered a team of people from Mumbai and Aamir was one of them. All of them were in the age group of 18 to 20. Both Aamir and Ashutosh Gowarikar came across as very bright and enthusiastic, energetic, focussed kids. And the choice was between Aamir and Ashutosh for the lead. Unfortunately Aamir landed up with a shaven head so we chose Ashutosh. We did a theatre workshop with all of them and Aamir even at that age was very focussed, very bright and intelligent and aware of cinema — not aware in the hazy sense but technically aware."

CHAPTER FOUR

Finding Himself

While doing *Holi*, Aamir Khan's first film, director Ketan Mehta noticed that he never projected himself beyond the requirement of the scene. "The ability to not project oneself beyond the need is also a great quality in an actor," said Mehta, "especially in most of these insecure actors. Upstaging, trying to get the better of the other actors, are some of the vices that creep in very early. I'm glad that Aamir has actually managed to retain that balance and not feel the need to do it. That shows a certain self confidence, a certain strength of character."

Aamir himself explained, "I've never used a role as a cathartic experience, for me that doesn't hold good at all. I approach my work as part of a group trying to tell a story. So there's the director who has a story to tell and I've to play my part in that process of telling the story in the correct way so that the story has a particular impact. And the joy I get out of it is to be able to convey that impact in an effective manner. Acting is not a cathartic experience for me at all.

Doing a particular film may be a traumatic experience at times, exciting at times but that's more a personal response. An opinion really. When I'm giving a shot, I'm trying to achieve what's best for the shot, not indulging in any personal trips."

Aamir has often been accused of "interfering" with directors [by outsiders, not by the directors themselves]. Ketan Mehta asserted, "Even when he was so young during *Holi,* he asked questions and discussed things — never abrasively but intelligently which I consider a strength. It's something I expect from an actor — to respond to the scene and the character with all his

Aamir and Nandita Das in 1947 Earth

intelligence and that quality Aamir certainly had. As an actor, he came across as restrained but very strong, very intense. He wasn't going overboard, that was not a problem that one ever had with him, there are few intelligent actors that one comes across, who you can talk with and who at least want to know and that is one of Aamir's strengths."

Meanwhile the actor was growing, his perceptions were sharpening and this was viewed sceptically by those filmfolk who were unused to being questioned at all. In Bollywood where compliments are the order of the day however fake they may be, it was unusual to have an actor who questioned illogical and irrational things. If his clothes did not fit, he would have something to say, if his dialogue appeared too corny he would put his foot down. This, while it made his directors more conscious when working with him, intrigued and irritated his co-actors who were unused to questioning the directors. Aamir once revealed, "In one film, I'm confronting my father and my dialogue goes 'Hey so and so…' here I'm supposed to address my father by his name and scream at him. Now no one ever does that. I can't imagine myself saying to my father 'Tahir Husain…you are wrong etc'. So I pointed this out to the director. It sounded completely ill fitting."

Rahul Khanna, his co-star in *Earth* felt that Aamir's so called perfectionism is a normal thing, "Those who criticise him must be people who don't have very high standards themselves hence they find his questions objectionable. I didn't find him doing anything that any thinking actor wouldn't or shouldn't do."

Prahlad Kakkad had a different perception of the actor, "Aamir takes himself very seriously in terms of his acting because he actually believes that he's not a good actor and to compensate for that he must put in that extra effort. He works damn hard. It can be fun working with him and it can be exasperating too." What makes Aamir difficult to digest is the stands he takes — again something that this multi-crore industry is unused to. Says Kakkad, "He'll walk away

With Mamta Kulkarni in 'Baazi'

from a position but won't compromise. So you can quit, but you can't persuade him to change his mind. If you think you can live with it then you can go with him blindly because he will adhere to his side of the bargain but he won't compromise one *naya paisa*."

The actor had reached the heights of stardom. He was already among the highest paid stars in the industry but he was also stepping carefully as if trying to find a firm footing. No achievement in Aamir's life was a one-off event. It became, for him a circumstance to be viewed in perspective and learn from. He was trying to imbue his life with a discipline and practicality which would be of help in his career. So earnest and real was his intent, that not only did he add to his own understanding of his life and profession, he was also equally sincere about sharing his insights and understanding. He learnt the virtue of meticulous pre-production work from

working with Deepa Mehta in *Earth* and used the same discipline in his production *Lagaan*. He found his *Dil Chahta Hai* director Farhan Akhtar also well equipped to make the film, so he invited John Mathew Mathan his *Sarfarosh* director to come and watch how *Dil Chahta Hai* and *Lagaan* were being made even though he did not have anything else with Mathan

With Sonali Bendre and John Mathew Mathan on the sets of 'Sarfarosh'

lined up. "His intention was to help me learn from these directors who had done all their pre-production work. I was very touched by his thoughtfulness. I find him a decent and sensitive person."

Aamir's sensitivity is yet another characteristic which, in this insensitive, back-stabbing industry, is viewed with caution. Farhan Akhtar analysed, "You can see he's sensitive because he gets hurt very easily but unlike others he's not only sensitive to his own needs but also to the project's needs. And if you haven't hurt him or maligned him in any way, he's amazingly supportive. I wanted him in *Dil Chahta Hai* because I admire him as an actor. He took this elder brotherly approach to Ritesh [the producer] and myself. Things often weigh you down when they don't go your way. He was always around to channelise all the good stuff and filter out the bad. He let us know in a very caring way, not forcefully but with great sensibility, that if he was required at any point of time for the betterment of the film, over and above his shooting dates, he would always be ready and available."

With Ajay Devgan in 'Ishq'

Vikram Bhatt revealed, "At times, he feels so intensely that his eyes brim with tears but he's not the kind to parade his feelings. In fact if he's been hurt, he'll let the wound fester, but not reveal it."

John Mathew was new when he was directing *Sarfarosh* and often so hassled being both producer and director that he would have willingly compromised with the creative aspect of the film. But Aamir sensing this, encouraged him to take his time and not make compromises that he would regret later. "He made it clear that on his part, he was always available and insisted that I should can a shot only when I was completely satisfied.

This is something I will never forget: his behaviour with me, a completely new director. One quality of his that stands out in my mind is his coolness in the face of adversity. When everything is going wrong and everyone is getting flustered, Aamir has the capacity to see things coolly and rationally and not get carried away by the circumstances. Quite remarkable really in someone who is not very old."

Yet these same directors had to wait long months, even years to gain access to Aamir and then convince him to listen to their scripts. Perhaps that is the biggest obstruction in the way of establishing any relationship with this so-called 'finicky' star. He has to be convinced before he agrees to anything. And he gives you complete freedom to convince him but to reach that point often takes so long that lesser mortals shy away from him. But after Aamir has made you jump through hoops in order to be convinced, once he accepts your sincerity he becomes completely loyal to you. Prahlad Kakkad says almost ruefully, "Aamir takes a stand and doesn't budge after that, but if the stand is in your favour, you have a good thing going!!"

Javed Akhtar reflected, "Aamir is a very resolved person. He has achieved an equation mentally and socially where there are no complications. I think it is his straightforward thinking and frank attitude that makes him so. Some people confuse his frankness for rudeness. So many people are rude and offensive and want to pass it off as being frank. Aamir's frankness is not rudeness, he is a very straightforward, simple person. His life is very organised. He doesn't get into what you'd call knee jerk reactions. He considers, weighs, thinks and then commits himself. Once he commits himself then he sticks to his commitments unlike some stars who make commitments everyday and never fulfill any of them."

Ketan Mehta clarified, "What people call his stubbornness is his strength. Aamir's intelligent and he's headstrong. In the sense that he makes a judgement of right and wrong, he values his own time and if somebody is not living up to expectation for x,y or z reasons he has a

right to speak his mind and he doesn't hesitate in doing so—and because such things don't happen here, Aamir becomes a rare character in this film industry of ours."

Anjum Rajabali, scriptwriter, revealed an interesting facet of the star, "One thing unusual in industry actors, that you find in him, is perception. He is able to look beyond the surface and catch the undercurrent. Therefore at the thematic level when you are having a discussion with him, it is very stimulating because there are very few people who look at things that way. The script requires a certain perceptiveness not only of human behaviour but also of its portrayal in a dramatic interplay. It is very stimulating to discuss it with him. One good thing about him is that when you narrate a script to him, he will catch it first intuitively, this restores my faith in the man, that he is not only intellectually inclined. Suppose somewhere there is a trip in the rhythm, he catches that intuitively even if he can't explain it immediately, he still gets into an argument about it and if you are patient enough to continue the discussion with him then over the next few minutes he is able to formulate a conscious argument. What follows then becomes a fruitful discussion. So one needs to exercise that patience. For this you've got to know him. He's not just being a star and expecting you to

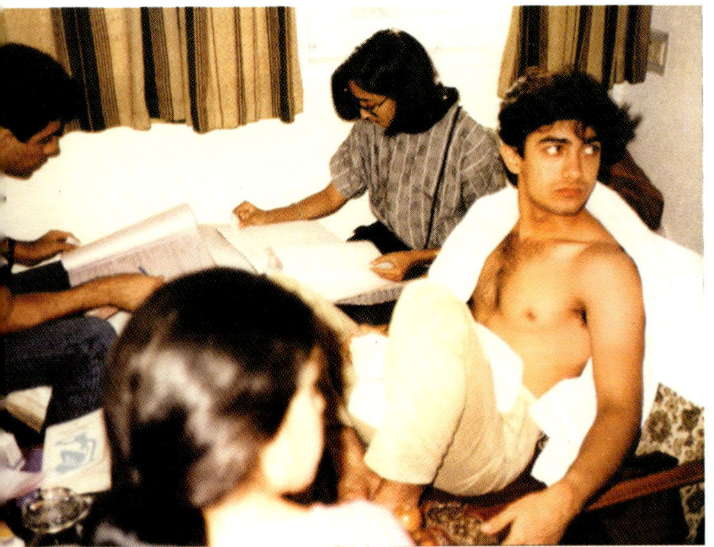

Relaxing with his cousins at his uncle Nasir Husain's house

listen to him. If you feel that, then you will lose out. On something which may be quite meritorious or at least worthy of consideration, that becomes for Aamir very essential because in the process of the discussion, his own thoughts begin to crystallise and you need to wait for that to happen."

So meticulous has Aamir become that he is often the butt of jokes of his co-stars and peers and they delight in recounting stories about his passion for detail and fussy questions. Shabana Azmi once recounted that Aamir was visiting her brother Baba Azmi and Shabana brought in a tea tray and started serving tea. Aamir and her brother were completely engrossed in some heated discussion when she interrupted and asked Aamir if he wanted sugar in his tea. He paused for a moment before replying in the affirmative and turned back to resume his discussion. A moment later Shabana interrupted and asked him how many spoons of sugar did he want. Aamir, interrupted in this fashion paused for a moment before replying And then he asked 'how big is the cup?' and after seeing the cup stated his requirement. Shabana Azmi related this story to everyone who would listen much to everyone's mirth.

Yet when I related this back to Aamir and asked him about it, he replied very naturally, "Baba and I were completely oblivious to what was going on, we were so engrossed in our discussion, so when Shabana kept interrupting and asking if I wanted sugar and then how much did I want etc, it took me some time to shift my attention to the questions she was asking, hence I paused. I wasn't being finicky but she was asking these questions so I was just being courteous and replying, if she hadn't asked but just given me the tea I would've drunk it."

Normal? Completely, but everyone approaches Aamir with a filter of 'difficult', 'fussy' etc. so everything he says and does is twisted to fit that mould. Rani Mukherjee, who adores him says, "I wish he wasn't so serious about everything. You want to shake him and say, "Take a chill pill Aamir!' "

With *Raghuvir Yadav in* 'Lagaan'

Having observed Aamir for about a decade, one has gathered that if anything puts him in an unforgiving rage it's unfairness of any kind. Other aberrations he lets go with an amused laugh but injustice he can not stomach. And in sync with this he behaves with great fairness to everybody making sure he never hurts or offends anyone's sensibilities. Raghuvir Yadav his co-actor in *Lagaan* stated categorically, "Aamir has drunk great gulps of humanity and it shows in every action of his. He is an admirable actor but he's an even more praiseworthy human being."

Prahlad Kakkad showed another facet of the warmth in Aamir when he recounted, "I remember during the Mumbai riots, I got a call from him at 2 am. He asked me if I knew anyone in the police. I asked him why and he said that his driver was stuck in a chawl which had been set afire and he wanted to get him out at any cost. I told him hold on I'll go with you. Believe me, this guy came in his car — we were on the highway with absolutely no one else in sight. This is the kind of commitment he has. Though I spoke with a lot of bravado, I was wondering what I was letting myself in for, but this guy was all there till everything had settled down."

However the same Aamir could not tolerate friend and co-star Juhi Chawla's unfair behaviour during the shooting of *Ishq* and allowed it to cause a rift in their decade long friendship, from the days when they were cast together in *Qayamat Se Qayamat Tak*. This falling apart between these two stars has been commented upon over the years and Aamir is seen as the unforgiving culprit and Juhi as the victim of his stubbornness. Yet knowing Aamir it was obvious that he would not digest unjustified behaviour. He once explained, "Yes I do appear unforgiving perhaps, but I'm not. If someone has hurt me, I do get upset but I am not permanently unforgiving. If the next person apologies and acknowledges that they've done something wrong. I'm willing to forget the whole thing but if someone is trying to get back to the old relationship just so they can get something out of me, then I'm not open to it. If they don't acknowledge their unfairness then I let it go. I have only two gears, forward and backward. I don't allow that person into my life again."

Ironically, Juhi Chawla did everything to regain lost ground. She sent him birthday wishes and congratulations at the birth of his daughter. The only thing she didn't do was to tell him that she was perhaps wrong. And Aamir being Aamir found it impossible to shut his eyes to that omission. What perhaps is not seen is that a man who can be so clear about his actions would also make an equally good friend. His claim to being emotional and passionate is not an

empty one, he is as emotional about being hurt as he is about hurting others.

One cannot help recalling how a character actor in one of his films borrowed a substantial amount of money from him, whining that he needed it to buy a house. Aamir gave him the loan. The borrower claimed that if he could show he had some money of his own to put into the house, then the bank would give him a loan for the rest. When the time came to repay, the actor disappeared. To surface months later with another story, 'Could Aamir please give him some more money otherwise he'd lose the bank loan as well as the house'. Despite his earlier experience with the actor, Aamir gave him yet another large loan. The man has neither returned the money nor ever contacted Aamir again!

With Juhi Chawla on sets of 'Ishq'

If Aamir has one quality which everybody generally and benevolently dislikes in him, it is his practical jokes. Ashutosh Gowarikar said, "His practical jokes are his worst quality!" He seems to get some peculiar pleasure out of strategising and executing elaborate practical jokes and everyone becomes his victim. Gracy Singh the new and rather subdued heroine of *Lagaan,* who had not even found her feet, while shooting for the film too fell for one of these. Once the two of them were shooting a romantic song atop a hill. Gracy was anxious and tense, besides that, the place was full of snakes and scorpions. The scene showed her sitting on the hill waiting for Aamir.

Sleeping with Junaid

"Suddenly something creepy went up my arm and I shrieked in terror only to find it was Aamir. Even in the heat and dust and difficult conditions of

Bhuj, he could still play these pranks!" recalled the surprised Gracy.

This penchant too was seen first in his childhood. Faisal his brother revealed, "Aamir and I used to wait for Farhat our younger sister to return from school. We have this clear view of the road from Mum's bedroom and as soon as we'd spot her, we'd take a bucket of water and dunk her as she reached the building entrance! She'd be furious but we always managed to take her unawares! All this was masterminded by Aamir."

With wife Reena, son Junaid and daughter Aira

Aamir himself says that in his marriage with Reena, he gets many opportunities to try his talent for practical jokes on her. "Once I was

shooting in Switzerland and the shoot wrapped up a few days before schedule. Reena used to call me at my hotel. I left a message with the reception that she should be told I was shooting late. And I hopped on to a flight and reached Mumbai. You can imagine how she did a double take when she opened the door and found me on the mat!"

Today though he admits ruefully, "My son Junaid has taken after me. In the way he thinks, he is exactly like me though in his looks he takes after Reena. Junaid knows I'm very fond of a particular chess board we have. Junaid and I play chess but I've warned him not to touch this board when I'm not there, it's very special, very rare and he knows I'm fond of it. Once when he was just three, we decided to play a board. I asked him to fetch it. He started laying the pieces on the board only to discover that one was missing. He looked at me frightened. I asked him if he'd been playing with it in my absence. He looked so crestfallen that I told him to look for it. He went through this elaborate act of looking for the piece then peering at my face for my reaction. After quite some time he opened his tiny palm and showed me that he was hiding the piece all the time! Just imagine he went through all this play acting for quite a while before revealing it." Aamir was being paid back in his own coin!

It is common knowledge that the affection he has for his family is very deep. He is closest to his cousin Nuzat, daughter of director Nasir Husain his uncle. Nuzat, an exceptional lady in every way has influenced Aamir's own sense of fairplay and uprightness. In fact when Aamir's uprightness was criticised in the industry as an aberration, it was Nuzat who reassured him, "Your time will come, people will realise what you stand for. Just do what you believe in." So close have the cousins always been that from childhood, they all live in each other's houses. Said Zeenat Husain, "The children would be in Nasir Sa'ab's house all the time and at mealtimes, they'd ring up and check what was cooked here. If they preferred what was cooked in their uncle's house they'd stay back and eat their meals there and often stay over. This affection has continued over the years."

Aamir adores his mother, "She's my mum, she is a wonderful person, and smashing to look at too!" he adds. His mother recalls fondly, "With his first pay cheque he bought me gold bangles and I was so taken aback."

Once when he was being accused of being emotionally involved with his leading lady, he replied unanswerably, "Why just my heroine, I've a great affection for Baba Azmi, the cinematographer too but no one highlights that because it's not a man/woman relationship.

With father Tahir Husain and brother Faisal Khan

I'm very happy in my marriage to Reena and don't feel the need for any other emotional sustenance."

All Aamir's strengths, convictions and principles came together and climaxed in his first film as producer — *Lagaan* and it paid him rich dividends.

Ketan Mehta analyses, "I saw *Lagaan* and thought that Aamir had seasoned as an actor. I'd say he has nerves of steel as a producer — it was a very courageous venture to invest so much of himself in — not in terms of money which is relative but it required a certain grave decision to take on this project. I'm glad that Aamir's was a courageous decision rather than a market driven tame decision. Anybody who doesn't want to balance the odds and does it because of a conviction, makes me feel proud. And I'm very proud of him. He has the courage necessary even in an environment of timid, scared people."

This is merely the beginning of another journey for this actor/producer who enjoys his stardom but does not operate from it. One can but say that fourteen years is a long time to receive his due but he has waited patiently for it. He reiterates, "I want to be the best loved star in the country!"

The rebel Bhuvan in 'Lagaan'

Chapter Five

The Actor and Filmmaker

As an actor, when he made his debut in *Qayamat Se Qayamat Tak,* Aamir Khan was seen as the typical chocolate faced hero with limited potential. He was too cute, too short, too small built to be anything but a romantic hero. What the public did not see was this newcomer's ambition and resilience. He was a survivor and he has worked hard at living down the first assessment made of him.

As is the Bollywood norm, filmmakers queued outside his door to sign him up immediately. Aamir, a novice, signed quite a few films — happy that other production houses were willing to take him on as an actor but in the rush he made some poor choices. Films like *Tum Mere Ho, Awwal Number, Diwana Mujh Sa Nahin,* or *Jawani Zindabad* did very little for his career. But in between the indifferent fare came *Dil Hai Ki Manta Nahin, Dil, Jo Jeeta Wohi Sikander, Hum Hain Rahi Pyar Ke, Andaz Apna Apna, Rangeela* — till he reached his peak with *Lagaan.*

In Rangeela *with Urmila Matondkar*

As one reviews his career graph, one can't help notice that he has tried to live down his bad choices by progressively becoming more careful before he signed a new film. He also came to the conclusion that signing so many films was not a good idea. He did not enjoy working in two or three films simultaneously, neither were the films doing well at the box office. He decided to choose his films with care and do only one or at best two films at a time.

When Indra Kumar's *Dil* succeeded, Aamir was not always happy with the way the dialogue read but his policy of complete commitment to the project at hand made him go along and be

convinced by the director. When Indra Kumar made *Ishq,* though the film hit the bull's eye at the box office, the inanity of the screenplay and dialogue made audiences realise that Aamir — the reliable, was still making mistakes. There were times when the director did not seem to give enough attention to the project and it was easy for the star to lose interest too. Aamir's own focus found its mark with directors like Dharmesh Darshan [*Raja Hindustani*], John Mathew Mathan [*Sarfarosh*] and even newcomers like Vikram Bhatt [*Ghulam*] and Ram Gopal Varma [*Rangeela*].

All these films were such massive hits that Aamir got himself the reputation of the star whose films were sure to succeed. He seemed to have found a formula for success; something no one has been able to do. Every newcomer director wanted Aamir in his film to ensure that it was a success. This meant he now had to deliver on the expectations he had raised. Strangely enough, he had driven himself into a corner where nothing but success would succeed. It was as if the actor was saying —'Expect nothing but the best from me.'

Ironically as an Aamir watcher, I've always wished that the actor had a larger, more varied repertoire of expressions — he seems to be limited, inhibited almost, by something one can not quite put a finger to, but he struggles hard to get past it. One often feels he does not let go enough, as if some inner driver holds the reins too tightly for him to break free. Ironically, his actions are all appropriate to the character he is portraying but his expression often isn't. *Dil Chahta Hai* asked more of him in the letting go department and to do him justice he tried his best but it still was not enough. This makes one realise that Aamir will still grow as an actor, still extract something from within to reach a height which perhaps he himself has not envisaged as yet.

Though his film *Lagaan* succeeded magnificently, it was perhaps *Dil Chahta Hai* that showcased a different side of the star. Which proves that Aamir works beautifully in tandem with a

In 'Dil Chahta Hai'

director who is clear about what he requires. So the first step he takes each time he signs a film is to tell the director that he is willing to do almost anything the he requires. By doing only one film at a time he shows that the filmmaker and his product have his full attention — not so ostensible is the fact that he expects the same from the filmmaker. This issue came to a head when during the making of *Ghulam,* director Mahesh Bhatt was directing more than one film at the same time. Aamir, himself so meticulous, could not bear the divided attention of the director and offered to quit. A controversy ensued which was later resolved by replacing the director with a newcomer, Vikram Bhatt.

Ghulam became one of the biggest box office successes ever with Aamir's role as Siddhartha being lauded by everyone. In fact the actor Aamir today has become the sum of the characters he has played in his hit films — the honest, unbending police officer of *Sarfarosh;* the couldn't care less but nevertheless sensitive *tapori* of

Rangeela; the honest to goodness taxi driver of *Raja Hindustani;* the careless Romeo of *Dil Chahta Hai* and of course the committed Bhuvan of *Lagaan.*

His commitment and focus have become the most outstanding characteristics of this star. His fight with the awards' juries for selling awards is seen as more of his integrity though he is in reality doing something that is very normal for him. It was these qualities that prompted friend Ashutosh Gowarikar to approach him with the story of *Lagaan.* Ashutosh with two failed films behind him, had just one overriding idea — that his next film should not be an apology, it should be on a huge canvas. Aamir heard his story and pooh poohed the idea. "It was good," he said, "but the chances of success were zero." His objections were — it was a period

film, nobody liked period films; it was set in rural India, at a time when people were going for feel good, urban and foreign locales. It was too expensive — to be shot in a village over a period of months was unrealistic. Gowarikar then approached Shahrukh Khan and Abhishek Bachchan believing that his story was so strong that any actor could carry it off, albeit differently. Both refused the film.

Gowarikar was not daunted but sat down and wrote the entire detailed script and approached Aamir again. After putting him off, Aamir relented and called him over for a story sitting — also inviting his parents to listen to the script. This time Gowarikar was ready for him. He enacted the whole four hour script going through each character's dialogues and actions in great detail. Something clicked in Aamir's mind and the project was on.

Aamir was fully aware that he could get producers for this film but he knew that the project was too expensive and an outside producer might interfere too much on the economics of it. So he decided to produce the film himself. After that there was no looking back. All his latent energy came to the fore as he played the dual role of producer/actor to the hilt. Work started on the selection of the cast and crew. The language spoken was to be Avadhi, so Javed Akhtar was roped in to write the lyrics. The music was to be by the incomparable A.R. Rahman. The leading lady took some time to decide — the choices were limited because not many actresses were willing to take up residence in Bhuj for over six months.

Reena, Aamir Khan's hitherto reclusive wife, took on the mantle of executive producer and hostess. Looking after the entire logistics and the arrangements of both the Indian and the foreign cast and crew was no mean job. After many auditions, Gracy Singh was chosen to play the leading lady — while the cricketing eleven were cast with much thought. At the location, a village was recreated and some miles away Aamir leased a whole building and converted it into a luxury hotel with food, laundry and medical services provided on the house. Each day,

With Gracy Singh in 'Lagaan'

a bus would fetch the entire cast and crew and take them to the location. The discipline was rigid and often quite intolerable. Gracy, unused to this kind of discipline was often in tears. She was also lonely and found the heat, cold and dust unbearable but since everyone was bearing the conditions stoically she had to do the same.

The shooting was difficult. The heat and dust ruined the make up, many times the cast and crew fell ill and had to be hospitalised. The director Ashutosh even had a stint directing the

film lying down due to a back problem. The entire cast went through myriad doubts wondering if they were crazy to have agreed to shooting in such conditions, catastrophes, illnesses, high tempers were the order of the shoot and it was Aamir's job to keep everyone happy and working. As if that was not taxing enough, the humorous side of the actor often came to the fore as he played his endless practical jokes on his co-stars. They even had a marriage on the sets — with Aamir giving the bride away.

The biggest irony was his having to switch roles from actor to producer and soothe the ruffled feathers of his wife when production expenses shot sky high. Aamir had to often argue in favour of the director to ensure that he could actuate his vision. The film not only overshot the budget, it overshot the time limit too. Finally it was over — Ashutosh hired a new editor Ballu Saluja to edit the massive film. Aamir was skeptical about his capacity to do justice to it but allowed Gowarikar the freedom to choose. Saluja did a fine job. Both Aamir and Ashutosh were present at every stage of the film's post-production.

They had even worked out a pre-release strategy. The star Aamir would speak to the Press last — the newcomers must give interviews first. The promos released on television were not titillating snippets, they were actual shots from the songs. Finally the film released to a stunning reception. Though there were vague rumours about the subject being cricket, no one quite knew what it was about. And it was the unexpected newness of the film that held everyone spellbound. Strangely enough, not one voice was heard saying anything derogatory about the film.

All the "opinions" about Aamir Khan came to a head — with the entire industry represented by his friends and foes congratulating him and wishing him luck. To cap it all, *Lagaan* became India's official entry to the Oscars. Each year when India is asked to send its entries to the Oscars, there are debates about the standard by which the films are sent, *Lagaan* was

the unanimous choice. Aamir commented., "If the principles on which the films are sent to the Oscars are not quite right we are all responsible — we can't blame anyone else. This time *Lagaan* has been sent and it has also got nominated among the first five — so it shows that the choice was correct."

Aamir Khan and Ashutosh Gowarikar with their wives in Los Angeles

All of India was watching as Aamir Khan and Ashutosh Gowarikar went to Los Angeles and made sure that the jury members actually saw their film. Earlier entries over the years had been so indifferent that jury members were used to skipping the Indian entries in their options. What the producer and director of *Lagaan* wanted was to ensure that even if their film did not win, it should get a fair viewing at least. They succeeded with some help from influential Indians abroad. And *Lagaan* found its place as one of the five nominees for the Oscar for a foreign film.

The entire country waited with bated breath for the actual ceremony to take place. Finally the day dawned, Ashutosh Gowarikar and Aamir were seated in the gathering as the Oscars were announced. Back home the entire *Lagaan* team gathered in Aamir's office to view the awards ceremony. The whole country waited for the early morning telecast of the Oscars ceremony

— only to hear that *Lagaan* had been pipped to the post by the Bosnia entry. Disappointment was quickly replaced by rationality. At least we had reached the end of the race!

They returned to a delightful welcome but the *Lagaan* hype was not over yet. For instance, several cricket matches across the country were arranged for the *Lagaan* team. Aamir participated in everything that would ensure that more people would see the film. Aamir still has found no time to start another film. He was invited to Locarno as a jury member, to the same festival, where last year his film won the Viewer's Choice Award. Most of the cast members have been savouring the result of the success of *Lagaan* in the form of better roles and more respect, while Aamir has become even more careful about what his next script should be. The overwhelming success of *Lagaan* has proved that hard work, commitment, fine detailing and team work does pay off. He said in hindsight, "For me every project is like climbing a mountain, reaching the top won't be as much fun as the journey itself. I like to make sure I enjoy every moment of the journey." And for him the real question now must be — what next?

Ashutosh Gowarikar with the Filmfare trophy for 'Lagaan' *- Best Feature Film*

3 2
OVERS

Filmography

1988	**Qayamat Se Qayamat Tak**	Juhi Chawla
1989	**Raakh**	
	Love Love Love	Juhi Chawla
	Tum Mero Ho	Juhi Chawla
	Dil Hai Ke Manta Nahin	Pooja Bhatt
1990	**Awwal Number**	Dev Anand, Ekta
	Deewana Mujh Sa Nahin	Madhuri Dixit
	Dil	Madhuri Dixit
	Jawani Zindabad	Farah
1991	**Afsana Pyar Ka**	Neelam
1992	**Daulat Ki Jung**	Juhi Chawla
	Isi Ka Naam Zindagi	Farah
	Jo Jeeta Wohi Sikander	Ayesha Jhulka, Pooja Bedi
	Parampara	Sunil Dutt, Vinod Khanna
1993	**Damini**	Rishi Kapoor, Meenakshi Sheshadri, Sunny Deol (guest appearance)
	Hum Hain Rahi Pyar Ke	Juhi Chawla
	Pehla Nasha	Deepak Tijori, Pooja Bhatt, Raveena Tandon

1994	**Andaz Apna Apna**	Salman Khan, Raveena Tandon
	Baazi	Mamta Kulkarni
1995	**Aatank Hi Aatank**	Rajnikant, Juhi Chawla
	Akele Hum Akele Tum	Manisha Koirala
	Rangeela	Jackie Shroff, Urmila Matondkar
1996	**Raja Hindustani**	Karisma Kapoor
1997	**Ishq**	Juhi Chawla, Ajay Devgan
1998	**1947-Earth**	Nandita Das
	Ghulam	Rani Mukherjee
1999	**Mann**	Manisha Koirala
	Rishtaa	Amitabh Bachchan, Madhuri Dixit
	Sarfarosh	Sonali Bendre, Naseeruddin Shah
	Mela	Faisal Khan, Twinkle Khanna
2001	**Laagan**	Gracy Singh
	Dil Chahta Hai	Priety Zinta